Is It Me?

By: Brent J. Baldwin

INTRODUCTION:

In the dim glow of the streetlight outside my window, I find solace. It's the time when the world is silent, and I'm left alone with my thoughts. But these thoughts, they're not comforting. They're a relentless storm, tearing through the fabric of my mind, leaving me with nothing but questions. Is it me? I often ask, my voice just a whisper in the darkness.

My name is Brent, Brent Baldwin. It's a name that used to carry a profound sense of pride, a symbol of the uniform I wore with unwavering honor. I've traversed multiple roles in my short 26 years of existence - a Navy veteran, entrepreneur, dedicated law enforcement officer, and a former firefighter. These roles have thrust me into a life where I've witnessed more in a few years than most people do in an entire lifetime.

My experiences have thrust me into the heart of life's fragility, where I've seen it teetering on the precipice of oblivion. I've stared down the barrel of danger, felt the adrenaline surge through my veins, and confronted death with a stoic resolve that leaves its mark, even if those scars are not visible to the naked eye. But it's not these external battles that weigh heaviest upon me; they're the ones that rage within the confines of my own mind.

The internal struggles I grapple with daily are far more daunting. They are the silent demons that accompany me through the corridors of my past, the memories that haunt my nights, and the questions that linger in the shadows of my thoughts. Who am I beyond the titles and roles I've played? What is the true measure of a man, and how do I reconcile the pieces of myself that I've left scattered across the years? These are the questions that echo in the depths of my soul, driving me to seek answers in the quiet moments when I'm alone, with my thoughts.

As I move forward, I'm determined to confront not only the dangers that lurk and wait outside but also the inner turmoil that threatens to consume me. It's a journey of self-discovery, an exploration of the meaning and purpose of my existence, and an attempt to make sense of the fragmented experiences that have shaped the person I am today. My name is Brent, Brent Baldwin, and this is the story of a man seeking to find himself amid the chaos of a life well-lived.

It's hard to pinpoint exactly when it started, this gnawing feeling in the pit of my stomach. Maybe it was the relentless nights on duty, the adrenaline fading away to leave me hollow and restless. Or perhaps it was the faces I couldn't save, their eyes haunting me in my dreams. Whatever the trigger, my mental health began to crumble, like a building worn down by time and neglect.

I isolate myself because in the deafening silence of solitude, I don't have to pretend. I don't have to wear the mask of bravery that the world expects from someone like me. The weight of my experiences presses down on me, making it hard to breathe, to function, to connect with the people around me. I withdraw, not out of choice, but out of necessity. Interactions become overwhelming, smiles become lies, and laughter feels foreign.

In these solitary moments, my mind becomes a battlefield. Why am I even here? I wonder…my fingers tracing the outline of old scars. The world outside moves on, but I'm stuck in a loop of despair and self-doubt. Why keep pushing? I ask myself, my gaze fixed on the ceiling. The goals I once had seem distant, like faded memories of a life I used to know. The drive that once propelled me forward has turned into an anchor, dragging me down into the depths of despair.

I think about the people in my life, the ones who love me despite my struggles. So and so, deserve better from me, I admit, my throat tightening with emotion. I see their concern, their frustration, and their helplessness reflected in their eyes. They want to understand, to help, but how can I explain something I can't comprehend myself? I can't give that to them, I acknowledge, my hands trembling as I write these words. It's not that I don't want to, but I feel like a shattered mirror, unable to reflect anything but broken fragments of who I used to be.

And I cannot explain it to them either, I confess, tears blurring the ink on the page. The fear of being misunderstood keeps me silent, keeps me locked within my own mind. I want to reach out, to scream for help, but the words get stuck in my throat, suffocated by the weight of my thoughts.

So, here I am, pouring my soul onto these pages, hoping that someone out there will understand. Hoping that my words will resonate with those who have felt the same suffocating darkness. This is not just my story; it's a raw, unfiltered account of what it's like to battle your own mind every single day.

Is it me? The question lingers in the air as I close my journal, the pen slipping from my fingers. I don't have the answers, not yet. But maybe, just maybe, by confronting these demons, by sharing this struggle, I can find a glimmer of hope amid the shadows. And perhaps, someone reading these words will find that glimmer too, illuminating the path toward understanding, acceptance, and healing.

One evening, as the sun dipped below the horizon, casting long shadows across my room, I decided. I couldn't continue living like this, drowning in my own thoughts, suffocated by the weight of my past. It was time to confront the darkness head-on, to seek out the help I so desperately needed.

With a newfound determination, I reached inward, seeking strength from the depths of my being. I began to unravel the tangled threads of my mind, exploring the scars that marked my soul. In the silence of self-reflection, I found courage. I acknowledged my fears, my doubts, and my pain. I embraced my vulnerability, understanding that it was not a weakness, but a source of immense strength.

I started to confront my past, the traumas that had cast long shadows over my present. Memories, long buried, resurfaced, demanding to be acknowledged. It was agonizing, revisiting the moments that had broken me, but with each painful step, I reclaimed a piece of myself. I forgave myself for the things I couldn't change, for the faces I couldn't save, and for the battles I couldn't win.

Through self-reflection, I began to see glimmers of hope amid the darkness. I discovered the resilience within me, the same resilience that had carried me through the most challenging moments of my life. I recognized the love that surrounded me, the unwavering support of my friends and family. And most importantly, I acknowledged my own worth, understanding that I deserved healing, happiness, and peace.

In the depths of my self-discovery, I found my voice. The words that had been trapped within me, suffocated by the weight of my thoughts, began to flow freely. I started to journal, pouring my innermost thoughts onto the pages of my notebook. It was liberating, expressing my emotions without judgment or restraint. Writing became my sanctuary, a place where I could be truly honest with myself.

As I delved deeper into my self-reflection, I realized that my experiences were not unique. There were others out there, battling similar demons, fighting similar battles. And in that realization, I found a sense of connection. I wasn't alone in my struggles. There was a community of people who understood the pain I felt, the isolation I experienced, and the questions that plagued my mind.

With this newfound understanding, I decided. I would share my story, not as a cry for pity, but as a beacon of hope. I would lay bare my vulnerabilities, my fears, and my triumphs. I would confront the darkness that had consumed me, and in doing so, I would shine a light for others who were still lost in the shadows.

And so, I embarked on this journey of self-discovery and healing, armed with nothing but my truth and the courage to speak it. This book, these words, are a testament to that journey. They are a testament to the power of self-reflection, of acknowledging our pain and embracing our strength. They are a testament to the resilience of the human spirit, the same spirit that resides within each-and-every one of us, waiting to be awakened.

As you read these words, know that you are not alone. Whatever battles you may be facing, whatever darkness may be clouding your mind, there is hope. Reach inward, confront your demons, and embrace your vulnerability. In your truth, you will find liberation. In your resilience, you will find strength. And in your story, you will find a connection.

This is my journey. This is my truth. And now, it is yours too.

Chapter 1: The Breaking Point

The sharp tang of the ocean air filled my lungs as I stood on the deck of the USS Valor, a formidable submarine that had become my second home. The familiar hum of the ship's engines resonated in my bones, a reassuring melody that had been the backdrop to countless journeys beneath the tumultuous waves of the sea. My name is Brent Baldwin, and I held the role of quartermaster, a position of leadership among my dedicated crewmates. Yet, as I stood there on that windswept deck, something had undeniably changed within me, something that defied no easy explanation or description.

It all began with a temporary assignment, a stint referred to as TAD, which took me away from the USS Valor and into a different world for a time. During those days and nights spent away from the submarine, I had been exposed to a set of circumstances and experiences that had left an indelible mark on my soul. When I eventually returned to the familiar confines of the submarine, my shipmates noticed an unmistakable shift in my demeanour. The spark that had once defined me, the unwavering commitment and enthusiasm that I had brought to every mission, had dimmed, replaced by a haunted look in my eyes.

My fellow sailors, the ones who had stood by my side through countless missions and trials, were quick to recognize that something was amiss. Their concern was palpable, their voices forming a collective chorus of worry and care. It was as though they could see the shadows that had taken residence within me, the echoes of experiences that had fundamentally altered the course of my being. They encouraged me to seek help, recognizing that I was facing a battle that transcended the usual challenges of life aboard a submarine.

As I stood on the deck of the USS Valor, I gazed out at the endless expanse of the sea, feeling its vastness mirror the depth of emotions and memories that had come to define my existence. I couldn't ignore the reality that something inside me had fractured, and the fragments seemed to drift in the vast sea of my consciousness like pieces of a shattered vessel. Those experiences on my temporary detachment had left me grappling with not just the rigors of the military but with a profound shift in my understanding of the world and my place in it.

For days, weeks, and even months, I had been away from the comforting steel embrace of the submarine. During that time, I had been exposed to situations that were worlds apart from the disciplined routines and tightly-knit camaraderie I had come to expect in my life as a submariner. The experience had been intense and challenging, pushing the limits of both my physical and emotional endurance. I had witnessed things that haunted my dreams, conversations that replayed in my mind like an unending loop, and the undeniable presence of danger that loomed around every corner.

When I returned, my shipmates noticed the transformation. It wasn't just the haunted look in my eyes; it was the heavy silence that seemed to have settled over my entire being. I was no longer the same Brent Baldwin who had ventured out on a TAD assignment. I had brought something back with me, something intangible yet undeniable. It was a weight that I struggled to carry, a burden that I couldn't easily articulate.

The concern of my fellow sailors was touching and genuine. They were more than just colleagues; they were my second family. Their understanding of the unique demands and challenges of submarine life meant that they were also the ones who could sense when something was amiss. They saw me for who I was, not just as a quartermaster but as a human being grappling with the aftermath of an experience that had shaken the very foundations of my identity.

As I navigated the labyrinth of my own thoughts and emotions, it became evident that the support I had received from my division and shipmates played an indispensable role in my healing journey. Their collective voice became the gentle yet persistent nudge that encouraged me to seek help, setting the wheels in motion for a transformation that extended far beyond the submarine's steel walls.

My division and shipmates had been with me every step of the way, recognizing that whatever had transpired during my time away was beyond the usual scope of our support systems. Their unwavering presence by my side was a testament to the bonds that had united us in this high-stakes environment. In those moments, it was clear that the camaraderie we had forged extended far beyond our professional duties; it was a brotherhood that transcended the ordinary.

However, as much as my division and shipmates stood beside me, there were those in higher positions who held different opinions. I vividly recall a day when I was summoned to the chief's quarters during chow hours. The atmosphere in the room was palpable with tension as the chiefs sat me down, surrounding me in an intimidating formation. Their words cut deep as they began to question my commitment to the submarine force and to my role as a sailor. It was a stern and unforgiving conversation, where they painted a stark picture of disappointment in my actions.

As the interrogation continued, their prying questions and accusations took a toll on my emotional well-being. The pressure and intensity of the moment became too much to bear. Tears welled up, and my body filled with a mixture of anger and distrust. I was emotionally overwhelmed, feeling isolated in the midst of my superiors who were, at that moment, more like judges.

The duration of this session felt like an eternity, stretching beyond an hour. The intensity of the encounter left a deep mark, both emotionally and mentally. It was a moment of reckoning, where I faced not only the consequences of my actions but also the weight of disapproval from those in positions of authority.

This chapter explores the profound contrast between the support I received from my division and shipmates and the condemnation I faced in the chief's quarters. It delves into the emotional turmoil I experienced during the intense conversation with the chiefs and how that moment served as a turning point, ultimately leading me to seek help. It was a juxtaposition of brotherhood and authority, a defining chapter in my journey of self-discovery.

The chapter continues to chronicle my journey of self-discovery and healing, which had now been set into motion by the contrasting experiences within the submarine. It highlights the uncharted territories within my own psyche that I began to explore, guided by the unwavering support of my division and shipmates.

As I reflect on these moments, I recognize that the USS Valor, once a place of unwavering purpose and commitment, had transformed into the backdrop for a new kind of journey. It was a journey that would teach me the significance of vulnerability and the strength in seeking help when needed. It became a profound lesson in the resilience of the human spirit and the enduring bonds of brotherhood that extended far beyond the confines of the submarine, echoing through the depths of my soul.

The open sea, with its boundless horizons and mysterious

depths, had become a metaphor for the vastness of the human experience. It was a reminder that we are all sailors on the sea of life, navigating its unpredictable currents and weathering its storms. But it was also a testament to the enduring power of community, the strength we find in one another when faced with challenges that seem insurmountable.

As I continued to heal and rebuild the shattered pieces of my own vessel, I carried with me the knowledge that the ocean, like life, could be both a source of trials and a wellspring of strength. And while the journey ahead remained uncertain, I faced it with a newfound resilience, knowing that I was not alone, that my shipmates would stand by my side, just as I would stand by theirs, as we sailed on together into the uncharted waters of the future.

Reluctantly, I acquiesced to the idea of seeing a therapist, grasping at the hope that perhaps this was the path toward solace and understanding. Little did I know that my journey toward healing would begin with an encounter that felt more like an interrogation than a therapy session. The therapist assigned to me was a stern and unyielding figure, a no-nonsense professional who seemed to have little time for niceties. As our sessions commenced, she wasted no time in diving headlong into the murky waters of my past, unearthing wounds I had long buried beneath the armour of stoicism.

Her words were like daggers, sharp and unforgiving, cutting through the carefully constructed facade I had built over the years to protect myself. There was no warmth or comfort in her presence, no soothing reassurances to ease the process of self-exploration. Instead, I felt as though my vulnerabilities were ruthlessly laid bare for ruthless scrutiny. In her relentless pursuit of the truth, her probing questions were like a relentless gust of wind that threatened to knock me off balance.

During those early sessions, I found myself teetering on the edge of an emotional precipice, a place of raw exposure where my emotions swirled like turbulent waters. Each session was a turbulent voyage into the uncharted territory of my inner self. I was unprepared for the tumultuous waves that crashed against the walls of my psyche, stirring up emotions I had long since suppressed.

As the therapist continued to press me, I became acutely aware of the fragility of the defences I had meticulously constructed. The armour that had served as a protective shield in the outside world seemed woefully inadequate in the face of her relentless inquiry. The walls I had carefully built over the years to guard my innermost fears and insecurities were crumbling under the weight of her questions.

In those initial sessions, I grappled with a potent mixture of emotions. I felt anger, frustration, and a sense of vulnerability I had never before experienced. I questioned the wisdom of opening up these long-sealed emotional vaults, fearing that I might be consumed by the very darkness I sought to confront. It was as if my therapist had unleashed a storm within me, one that raged with the force of suppressed memories and long-buried pain.

Despite the tumultuous journey, I also experienced moments of unexpected clarity. The therapist's unyielding approach forced me to confront truths I had long denied, to acknowledge the depths of my own pain, and to sift through the complex web of emotions that had entangled me for years. As I navigated the maze of my past, I began to see glimmers of understanding, faint beacons of hope that suggested healing might be possible.

The therapy sessions were not easy. They were, in fact, some of the most challenging experiences I had ever faced. Yet, as we delved deeper into the recesses of my psyche, a transformation was taking place. I realized that healing was not a linear path but a tumultuous, meandering journey. It was a process of confronting the shadows within me, acknowledging the pain, and gradually learning to find meaning in the chaos.

I discovered that the therapist's relentless questioning was not an attack but a deliberate strategy to peel away the layers of protection I had wrapped around myself. Her stern demeanour was a reflection of her commitment to guiding me through the labyrinth of my own emotions. As we progressed through the sessions, I began to appreciate the unflinching support she provided, a support that demanded that I confront my inner demons with unwavering courage.

The therapy sessions were not about finding quick fixes or easy solutions. Instead, they were about delving into the depths of my own psyche, confronting the tangled emotions that had long held me captive, and ultimately finding a path toward self-acceptance and healing. It was a journey that pushed me to the limits of my emotional endurance, but in the process, I uncovered a wellspring of strength and resilience I had never known I possessed.

While the therapist's approach remained unyielding, I gradually learned to appreciate the depth of her commitment to my well-being. She was not there to coddle me or to provide comforting platitudes. Instead, she was a guide, a navigator through the turbulent waters of my own mind. The storm she had unleashed within me gradually gave way to a sense of clarity and purpose.

Over time, the sessions became less of a battleground and more of a sanctuary for self-discovery. The tumultuous waves of emotion began to subside, replaced by a sense of calm and understanding. The process of healing was far from complete, but it had begun, and I was no longer teetering on the precipice of emotional collapse. Instead, I was standing on the threshold of a new chapter in my life, one in which I would be able to confront my past, embrace my vulnerabilities, and ultimately find solace and understanding on the other side of the tempestuous journey I had embarked upon.

The breaking point came swiftly and unexpectedly. One evening, overwhelmed by the weight of my thoughts, I found myself consumed by a darkness so profound that it threatened to swallow me whole. The therapist's probing, had **resurrected** buried traumas, scars that I had tried so hard to forget. In that moment of despair, I admitted to myself something I hadn't dared to acknowledge before – I was spiralling, drowning in the depths of my own mind.

The realization of my own vulnerability terrified me. I reached out, desperate for help, and within hours, I was admitted to the hospital. The sterile surroundings of the psychiatric ward became my reality for the next three days, a stark contrast to the confines of the submarine I had called home.

The hospital, with its regimented routine, it was a world far removed from the solitary existence I had carved for myself within the confines of my living room, where I would sit for hours of the night with an 18-pack of beer and video games, seeking to drown the cacophony of mental struggles that had plagued me. I had reached a point where alcohol had become both a crutch and a coping mechanism, an attempt to numb the relentless storm of thoughts that raged within my mind. But the very substance I had turned to for solace had now become the source of my distress, prompting the nurses to maintain a vigilant watch over me.

The hospital staff, in their dedication to my well-being, would enter my room like clockwork, every 30 minutes on the mark, to monitor my vital signs and ensure that my body wasn't shutting down due to the withdrawal from alcohol. The regimen of checks was a reminder of the depths to which my struggles had led me. It was as if my body, much like my mind, had reached a breaking point, and I was teetering on the precipice of a physical and emotional abyss.

The experience of the hospital was a disorienting one. The days were a blur of medications and counselling, a relentless confrontation with the intensity of my emotions. The therapy sessions provided a safe space for me to unravel the tangled web of my own thoughts and experiences. It was in these moments of vulnerability that I began to confront the harsh truth – my mind, once my greatest asset, had become my greatest enemy.

The therapist at the hospital, in contrast to my first encounter with therapy, exhibited a gentle and empathetic approach. Her compassionate guidance encouraged me to express the pain and fear that had long been buried beneath layers of self-imposed stoicism. The tumultuous waves of emotion that had threatened to engulf me were gradually brought under control, allowing for a sense of equilibrium to emerge.

The hospital's support groups were a revelation, allowing me to connect with others who were navigating similar battles. The stories of resilience and recovery, shared by fellow patients, served as beacons of hope in the darkest of times. The community of individuals struggling with their own demons offered a profound sense of solidarity, a reminder that I was not alone in my fight against the encroaching darkness.

Despite the turbulence of emotions, I began to sense the faint glimmers of healing. The hospital had provided the structured environment I needed to begin the process of unearthing and addressing the traumas that had laid siege to my psyche. The therapy and support groups became my lifelines, offering me the tools and insights I required to navigate the treacherous waters of my own mind.

The hospital stay was a brief yet profoundly transformative chapter in my life, one that marked the beginning of my journey toward healing and self-acceptance. It was a journey that I knew would be arduous, filled with uncertainties and challenges. Yet, as I emerged from those sterile hospital walls and re-entered the world, I carried with me the knowledge that I was no longer alone in my struggle. The hospital had provided me with the tools and support I needed to confront my demons and to embark on a path of recovery. The nurses' vigilant watch over my physical well-being had been a reminder of the depths to which I had fallen, but it was also a testament to the resilience of the human spirit, a spirit that could emerge from the darkest of moments to find solace and understanding on the other side of the tempestuous journey I had embarked upon.

Upon my release, my life took an abrupt turn. The Navy, an institution I had dedicated years of my life to, medically discharged me. The diagnosis of obsessive depression and anxiety disorder became a label, one that I carried with me like a burden. The uniform that had once defined me was replaced by civilian clothes, and I found myself adrift, severed from the sense of purpose that had guided me for so long.

As I faced the daunting prospect of civilian life, I grappled with a sense of loss and identity crisis. Who was I without the Navy? The transition was far from smooth, marked by moments of profound isolation and self-doubt. I struggled to find my footing in a world that seemed alien and indifferent.

The wounds I carried, both visible and invisible, shaped my interactions with the world. I withdrew from those around me, unable to bridge the gap between the person I used to be and the person I had become. The fear of judgment and misunderstanding kept me silent, trapped within the confines of my own thoughts.

In the midst of my struggles, I clung to the fragments of my former self. The memories of camaraderie aboard the submarine, the adrenaline-fueled operations, became a bittersweet reminder of a life that was now out of reach. I yearned for the sense of belonging, the unwavering support of my shipmates, but it felt like a distant dream.

The weight of my diagnosis hung heavy on my shoulders, a constant reminder of my perceived shortcomings. I questioned my worth, my abilities, and whether I would ever find my purpose again. The future seemed bleak, a daunting landscape of uncertainties and unanswered questions.

And yet, within the depths of my despair, a glimmer of hope persisted. It was a fragile flame, flickering amidst the darkness, but it refused to be extinguished. I knew, deep within me, that I couldn't let my struggles define the rest of my life. I had faced battles before – on the submarine, in the Navy – and I was determined to face this one head-on.

With the support of my family and a few trusted friends, I embarked on the challenging journey of recovery.

It wasn't an easy road. The scars of my past ran deep and confronting them was a painful process. I started to untangle the knots of my emotions. I learned coping mechanisms and strategies to navigate the overwhelming waves of anxiety that threatened to engulf me.

As I delved into the roots of my obsessive depression and anxiety disorder, I began to understand the intricacies of my own mind. The therapist's approach was gentle, a far cry from the harsh interrogation I had experienced before. Together, we explored the traumas of my past, acknowledging the pain without judgment.

In the safety of therapy, I found my voice. I shared the depths of my despair, the moments of hopelessness that had plagued me for so long. The therapist listened, her presence a beacon of understanding in my darkest moments. It was in those sessions that I started to piece together the fragments of my shattered identity.

Recovery wasn't linear. There were setbacks, moments of despair that threatened to undo my progress. But I persevered, drawing strength from the resilience that had carried me through the Navy.

Slowly but surely, I started to rebuild my life. I found solace in creative outlets – music, videos– channelling my emotions into videos. The process was cathartic, allowing me to express the turmoil within me in a tangible form. I also rekindled my love for nature, finding peace in the quiet serenity of the outdoors.

With time, the fog of despair began to lift. The glimmer of hope that had persisted within me grew stronger, illuminating the path toward healing. I embraced the uncertainties of civilian life with a newfound resilience, determined to redefine my sense of purpose.

Through therapy and self-reflection, I started to challenge the negative beliefs that had held me captive for so long. I questioned the judgments I had placed on myself, replacing them with words of kindness and self-compassion. It was a gradual process, one that required immense patience and self-love.

As I embraced my vulnerabilities, I found unexpected strength. I shared my story with others, breaking the silence that had kept me isolated for so long. The act of opening-up became a form of empowerment, a declaration that I was more than my diagnosis. I was Brent Baldwin, a survivor, a warrior who had faced the darkness and emerged stronger on the other side.

The journey was far from easy, but it was transformative. I learned that asking for help wasn't a sign of weakness, but an act of courage. I discovered the power of self-acceptance, of embracing the complexities of my being without judgment. And most importantly, I found my purpose not in the uniform I once wore, but in the resilience of my spirit.

This was my story – a story of struggle and resilience, of despair and hope. And as I stepped into the next chapter of my life, I did so with a newfound sense of purpose. The scars of my past were a testament to my strength, a reminder that I had faced the darkness and emerged into the light.

As I looked toward the future, I knew that the road ahead wouldn't be easy. There would be challenges, moments of doubt and fear. But I faced them with a courage that had been forged in the crucible of my struggles. I was no longer defined by my diagnosis; I was defined by my resilience, my determination to live a life filled with meaning and purpose.

And so, with each step forward, I carried with me the lessons of my past. I had faced the storm and survived. I had navigated the depths of my own mind and emerged stronger. The journey was far from over, but I faced it with a newfound sense of hope – a hope that whispered, even in the darkest of moments, that I was not alone, that I was worthy of love and belonging.

This was my story, a story of survival, of triumph over adversity. And as I embraced the uncertainties of the future, I did so with a heart full of gratitude. Gratitude for the strength within me, for the love of those who had stood by my side, and for the unwavering belief that no matter how daunting the journey, I could navigate its depths.

And so, with a deep breath and a heart full of courage, I took the first step into the next chapter of my life, ready to embrace whatever lay ahead.

Chapter 2: The Illusive Normalcy

Returning to civilian life after my dedicated service in the Navy was a challenging and uncertain transition. The structured routines and unwavering discipline of military life had been a constant in my life, offering clear guidelines and purpose. However, as my time in the Navy came to an end, I found myself standing at the threshold of civilian existence, where the path ahead was uncharted and undefined.

In those early days of my civilian life, I was desperately in search of a sense of familiarity, a place where I could find solace and rekindle the spirit of camaraderie that had been a cornerstone of my military experience. It was then that I discovered an unexpected refuge in the halls of the fire department.

For me, the fire department was not just a workplace or a career choice; it was a true home, a sanctuary that had shaped my identity even before I donned the uniform. During my high school years, the fire station had been more than just a place I visited; it had been my abode. I lived within its walls, dedicating my time and energy to volunteering during the nights and after school. It was my way of giving back to the community that had nurtured me and my way of satisfying a deep-seated desire to help those in need.

Those years spent at the fire station had been profoundly formative, instilling in me a sense of purpose and a dedication to service that would become the bedrock of my character. The fire department was not merely a place of work; it was an extension of my being, a place where I found inspiration and a sense of belonging. The bonds I forged with my fellow volunteers were unbreakable, echoing the camaraderie I had shared with my fellow sailors during my military service.

It was amidst the flames and chaos of firefighting that I encountered individuals who would later play pivotal roles in shaping my destiny. It was through these newfound friends that I was introduced to the world of law enforcement, a realm that beckoned with a promise of new challenges and opportunities to serve my community in a different capacity.

Their stories, filled with dedication, sacrifice, and the pursuit of justice, ignited a passion within me that I hadn't anticipated. The idea of making a meaningful difference in the lives of my fellow citizens resonated deeply with me, driving me to explore this new path.

Encouraged by their narratives, I made the life-altering decision to apply at the Angelina College Police Academy. The desire to contribute meaningfully to society once more fueled my determination, and I embarked on this new journey with a sense of purpose that was as unwavering as it was deeply rooted in my experiences.

The days at the police academy were intense and challenging, pushing both my physical endurance and mental acuity to their limits. I was unwavering in my dedication to excel, pouring myself into the training with unrelenting determination. The rigorous hours of study, the physically demanding drills, and the high-stress simulations became the centrepieces of my life, testing my limits and forging my character in the fires of adversity.

However, there was a significant additional challenge that I undertook during my time at the academy. While I was diligently attending classes and engaging in rigorous training, I was also working full-time at a county jail on the night shift. The sheer demand of this dual commitment was relentless. Each day, I would rise before 6 a.m. and embark on the lengthy drive to Lufkin, where my classes and training awaited me. After a full day of academic and physical exertion, I would then turn around and drive back to Lufkin for additional classes, a round trip that spanned several hours.

This relentless schedule often left me sleep-deprived and pushed my physical and mental capacities to their limits. I would frequently find myself in the precarious situation of having gone without sleep for extended periods. With the demanding rotation of my work shifts, there were three days a week when sleep became a luxury I couldn't afford. It was a strenuous juggling act that required immense dedication and endurance.

The turning point came when the strains of this dual commitment began to manifest in my safety on the road. I experienced too many close calls and one particularly harrowing encounter with a horse standing in the middle of the road, which served as a stark reminder of the dangers of my sleep-deprived state. It was then that I made the difficult but necessary decision to focus solely on my academy training in the last few weeks of the program, putting my full-time job at the county jail on hold. This choice was made not out of a sense of defeat, but as a testament to my commitment to becoming a safer driver and to fully engage in the rigorous training required to excel in law enforcement.

My journey, from the military to the fire department, and finally to the police academy, had been marked by unwavering dedication, resilience, and the pursuit of a higher calling. The path had been fraught with challenges and uncertainties, but it was a path I embraced with open arms, guided by the spirit of service that had been ingrained in me from my early days in the fire department. The unrelenting commitment to my training and the pivotal decision to prioritize my safety on the road were emblematic of the sacrifices I was willing to make in my quest to serve my community with honor and dedication.

Embarking on my law enforcement career, I was filled with a profound sense of purpose. Each day felt like a chance to make a positive impact, to protect and serve my city. I approached my duties with unwavering dedication, often arriving at work early and volunteering additional hours to combat the rampant drug issues that plagued our streets.

My partner, a steadfast presence by my side, was not just a colleague but a true confidant. Together, we formed a formidable team, working tirelessly to seize illegal substances and apprehend those who threatened the safety of our community. The bond we shared extended beyond the professional realm, transcending the confines of the workplace. He was more than just a fellow officer; he was a genuine friend, someone with whom I shared a unique camaraderie born of shared trials and triumphs.

In the rare moments of respite we managed to carve out from our demanding roles, we found solace and rejuvenation in a shared passion for fishing. Those outings, often by the banks of tranquil lakes or meandering rivers, became our escape from the relentless challenges and stresses of our roles as law enforcement officers. Casting lines into the waters, we sought not only to catch fish but to find moments of serenity amid the chaos we encountered on the job.

One particular day, however, the tides of anticipation took an unexpected turn. An eagerly anticipated fishing trip with my partner dissolved into disappointment when he had to cancel at the last minute. As I grappled with this sudden change in our plans, my phone rang – the call was from my supervisors, and they were summoning me into work on my scheduled day off.

The phone call filled me with a surge of excitement and curiosity. It was unusual to be called in on a day that had been meant for rest and relaxation. With a sense of anticipation, I wondered if my unwavering dedication and tireless commitment to the job were finally being recognized. Perhaps it was to be a well-deserved promotion or a raise, a testament to the sacrifices I had made to protect and serve my community.

My heart pounded with a mix of apprehension and hope as I made my way to the station. The journey was a short one, but the minutes seemed to stretch endlessly, my thoughts a whirlwind of anticipation. I was filled with a potent blend of emotions, ready to face whatever news awaited me.

Little did I know that the events about to unfold would not only test my dedication to the job but also challenge the very core of my character. The sudden summons was the prelude to a pivotal moment in my law enforcement career, one that would test not only my professional resolve but also the bonds of friendship that had been forged in the crucible of our shared experiences.

But what awaited me at the precinct shattered my optimism. A case file, thick with allegations stemming from a past relationship, was slapped onto the table before me. It was a false and malicious accusation, a fabrication that had the potential to not only jeopardize my law enforcement career but also to tarnish my personal reputation. For two agonizing years, I found myself thrust into the relentless scrutiny of an criminal investigation, my life placed under an unforgiving microscope as I waged a tireless battle to prove my innocence.

The toll of those long and gruelling years was immeasurable. I had to endure the weight of suspicion and the burden of having my actions and character dissected in painstaking detail. The clouds of doubt hung heavily over my head as I navigated the treacherous waters of the investigation. It felt as if my entire world had crumbled, and I was left grappling with the wreckage of my dreams and aspirations.

When the truth finally emerged, I was exonerated, but the damage had been done. My law enforcement license had lapsed during the investigation, rendering me at a crossroads. I had a choice to make, one that would define the trajectory of my life. I could have opted to pursue legal action against my accuser, seeking retribution for the unjust suffering I had endured. However, I chose to take a different path – a path of forgiveness and moving forward.

Deciding to be the bigger person, I made the difficult but liberating choice to let go of the anger, bitterness, and resentment that had built up during those tumultuous years. Instead of dwelling on the painful past, I directed my focus toward rebuilding my life. My dreams of a lifelong career in law enforcement had been irrevocably shattered, but I refused to let this devastating setback define me.

Embracing the spirit of resilience that had carried me through the Navy and my law enforcement career, I embarked on a new journey – one that would lead me down a radically different path. This was a journey that would steer me toward entrepreneurship and a more conventional job.

Starting my own business became my beacon of hope in a world that had once been filled with the optimism of a promising law enforcement career. It represented a fresh start, a chance to channel my energy and determination into something positive, and to breathe new life into my sense of purpose. The process of building and running my own enterprise was a terrain of challenges that was vastly different from my experiences in the military and law enforcement.

But with the same fervour and determination I had brought to those previous chapters of my life, I plunged headlong into the world of entrepreneurship. I wasn't just learning the ropes; I was grasping them with an unwavering grip. The pursuit of business success became my new mission, and I was determined to excel in this endeavour with the same unrelenting spirit that had carried me through my past challenges.

As I navigated the complexities of running my own business, I found a profound sense of fulfillment. The challenges were different, and the terrain was unfamiliar, but the resilience I had homed in the face of adversity served me well. Every obstacle became an opportunity to learn, to adapt, and to grow. It was in the relentless pursuit of entrepreneurial success that I discovered the immense power of perseverance and the boundless potential of the human spirit to overcome even the most devastating setbacks.

In the midst of my entrepreneurial journey, I discovered a profound and revitalized appreciation for the simpler pleasures that life had to offer. These were the moments that I had once taken for granted, the gentle respite from the relentless demands of my previous careers. Now, I savored the tranquility of quiet mornings, my hands wrapped around a comforting cup of coffee, as I watched the world awaken with a sense of serenity.

Life had changed, and so had my perspective. I found joy in the laughter shared with friends and family, recognizing the importance of these connections that brought warmth and comfort into my life. The scars of my past still lingered, etching themselves into the fabric of my being, but I no longer viewed them as burdens. Instead, I wore them as badges of honor, reminders of the battles I had fought and the strength I had discovered within myself.

Amid the challenges and unexpected twists that had characterized this new chapter of my life, I discovered a semblance of normalcy. The sense of purpose that had once been synonymous with my military and law enforcement careers now found its expression in the everyday moments – in the smiles exchanged with strangers, in the satisfaction that came from a job well done, and in the quiet moments of self-reflection.

Looking back on my life's journey, I realized that it had been unpredictable, often throwing curveballs when I least expected them. Yet, I had learned that resilience was not solely about bouncing back from adversity; it was also about the capacity to adapt and find new avenues for growth. The path I had envisioned might have been altered, but the essence of who I was remained unbroken.

As I moved forward into the unknown, I carried with me the profound lessons of my past. I had learned the importance of forgiveness, the power of resilience, and the value of embracing change. These lessons had been hard-won, etched into the fabric of my existence. With each step, I embraced the elusive concept of normalcy, understanding that it was not about the absence of challenges but about how I faced and navigated them. And so, with a heart full of courage and a spirit that was unyielding, I welcomed the uncertainties of the future, ready to confront whatever lay ahead with the same indomitable spirit that had carried me through life's most trying moments.

Chapter 3: Embracing Light in Unexpected Places

In the midst of my struggles, I stumbled upon a ray of sunshine that would change the course of my life – Nicole. She was not just the love of my life; she was the most beautiful and sweetest human being on this planet. Her kindness knew no bounds, and her love was a force that could conquer any darkness. To me, she was not just a partner; she was a sanctuary of understanding, a safe harbor where my turbulent thoughts found solace.

Nicole was not just my partner; she was the best mom in the world. Her love for her son and our daughter knew no bounds, and she embraced her role with a grace that inspired me. Her unwavering support became my lifeline, a reminder that amidst the chaos of my thoughts, there existed a sanctuary of love and acceptance.

The love we shared became a testament to the transformative power of connection. In her eyes, I found a reflection of my worth, a reminder that I was more than the sum of my struggles. Despite the darkness that clouded my mind, she saw the light within me, a light that had dimmed but had never fully extinguished. Her belief in me became a source of strength, a lifeline I clung to in my moments of despair.

Yet, as much as I cherished her presence, a shadow of guilt loomed over me. My depression, anxiety, and intrusive thoughts had become a storm that swept through our lives, leaving a trail of uncertainty and pain. It was a burden I carried with a heavy heart, watching as my family weathered the tempest of my mind. The question that haunted my thoughts, like a relentless echo, was "Is it me?" Was I the root cause of the storms that raged within our home? Was my struggle with mental illness the poison that seeped into the cracks of our happiness?

Navigating the intricacies of parenthood became a Herculean task in the face of my mental health battles. The simplest of tasks felt like climbing mountains, and the weight of my thoughts often pulled me into the abyss of despair. I longed to be the best dad, to provide a stable and loving environment for our children, but the darkness within me threatened to overshadow my intentions.

The pain of witnessing the impact of my mental health on my family was a wound that cut deep. I watched as friendships withered and relationships crumbled under the weight of my struggles. The self-imposed isolation became a fortress, a feeble attempt to shield my loved ones from the storm within. Yet, in my isolation, I found no solace – only the haunting echo of my own thoughts, questioning my worthiness of love and companionship.

In Nicole's eyes, I saw the reflection of my pain. She witnessed the battles I fought within the labyrinth of my mind, and her empathy became a beacon of hope. Yet, even in her understanding, I couldn't escape the gnawing question – "Am I enough?" Was my love sufficient to compensate for the challenges I brought into our lives? Did my struggles diminish my worthiness of the love she so freely gave?

Each day was a war, a battlefield where my desire to be a loving partner and father clashed with the relentless onslaught of my mental demons. And amidst the chaos, the question that echoed loudest was, "Is it me?" Was I the puzzle piece that didn't fit, the discordant note in the symphony of our family?

Despite the storms, there were moments of respite – moments when our laughter echoed through the walls of our home, moments when I held our daughter in my arms and felt an overwhelming surge of love, moments when Nicole's smile became a glimmer of hope in the darkness. It was in these moments that I found the strength to keep fighting, to believe that amidst the storm, there existed the possibility of a calm sea.

Nicole's unwavering love became a lifeline, a reminder that I was not alone in my struggles. She stood by me, weathering the storms with a grace that left me in awe. Her kindness became a source of inspiration, urging me to believe that I was deserving of love despite my flaws.

Yet, even in the midst of her love, the question lingered –
"Is it me?" Would I ever be enough for her and our
children? Would my battles with mental health forever cast
a shadow over our family?

In my moments of despair, I looked at Nicole, her eyes
filled with love and understanding, and I realized that
perhaps the answer to my question was not rooted in my
struggles but in the resilience of our love. Despite the
storms, we clung to each other, navigating the turbulent
seas together. It was in our togetherness that I found a
glimmer of hope, a belief that love had the power to
weather even the fiercest of storms.

As I held our daughter in my arms, her innocent eyes filled
with trust, I made a silent promise – a promise to fight, not
just for my own sake but for the sake of the beautiful souls
who depended on me. I would battle the darkness within
me, not because I was free from fear but because I refused
to let fear define me.

And so, amidst the question that haunted my thoughts, I found the strength to embrace the uncertainty. Perhaps the answer to "Is it me?" was not a declaration of inadequacy but a reminder of the battles I had fought and the resilience I had displayed. In the eyes of my family, I was not just a man struggling with mental health; I was a warrior, fighting a battle that tested the very core of my being.

As I looked at Nicole, her smile a beacon of hope, I realized that the question that had plagued my thoughts was not a condemnation but a catalyst for growth. It was a question that pushed me to confront my demons and emerge stronger. It was a question that urged me to seek help, to lean on the love of my family, and to believe that amidst the storms, there existed the possibility of a new dawn.

In the embrace of our family, I found the courage to face the darkness within me. Nicole's love became a sanctuary, a refuge where my scars were embraced and my flaws were celebrated. And as I held her hand, I knew that together, we would navigate the complexities of life, finding strength in the love that bound us together.

Chapter 4: Reflections in the Mirror

In the depths of my struggle, I found myself embarking on a profound and soul-searching journey of self-reflection. This was not just a battle against my own mind; it was a quest to understand the intricate web of thoughts and emotions that relentlessly consumed me. In those moments of solitude and introspection, I delved deep into the recesses of my soul, searching for meaning amidst the chaos that had threatened to define me.

Section 1: The Mirror of Self

Facing my own reflection, both in the literal sense and in the metaphorical reflection of my life's choices, became a daunting task. The eyes that stared back at me in the mirror held within them a universe of pain and questions, each line and crease on my face etching a story of silent struggle. It was in those moments of vulnerability and self-examination that I began to realize the profound importance of self-acceptance.

I recognized that my mental illness was not a flaw, but rather a significant facet of my being. It was a part of the complex tapestry that made me who I was, woven from the threads of my experiences, my traumas, and my resilience. I traced the intricate origins of my anxiety and depression, daring to delve into the deep recesses of my psyche to understand their roots.

The journey was like excavating a buried city, uncovering the layers of history that had shaped my worldview. I revisited the moments of my past, from the scars of my formative years to the disappointments of adulthood, seeking the key moments and experiences that had left indelible marks on my emotional landscape.

As I unearthed these memories and explored the complex

interplay of events and emotions, each revelation brought with it a poignant mix of sorrow and relief. Sorrow, as I confronted the battles I had fought in silence, the moments when I had grappled with my inner demons without reaching out for help. But also, a profound sense of catharsis that came with acknowledging the truth. The truth that I was not alone in my pain, that there was a context to my struggles, and that understanding these origins was the first step on the path to healing.

Section 2: Echoes of Shared Struggles

In my unwavering quest for understanding, I embarked on a journey that led me to a profound connection with others who, like me, had weathered the relentless storms of mental illness. Their stories became a symphony that harmonized with mine, creating a chorus of shared struggles, and together, we found solace. The friend who had battled anxiety, the colleague who faced the crippling weight of depression, the neighbour who grappled with intrusive and unrelenting thoughts – in their experiences, I glimpsed reflections of my own battle.

As I listened to their narratives and bore witness to their vulnerabilities, a profound realization washed over me. It was a revelation that struck a chord deep within my soul, one that would forever change the course of my own journey. I discovered the universality of human suffering, a revelation that transcended the boundaries of age, race, or social status. It was a profound testament to the fact that we were all bound together not just by our unique challenges, but by the incredible strength and resilience that resided within us.

In these shared experiences, I found a sanctuary, a place of understanding and camaraderie that had previously eluded me. The knowledge that I was not alone in my struggles became a lifeline, a source of hope that would guide me through even the darkest of nights.

Section 2.1: The Friend with Anxiety

Among those who shared their stories, I met a friend who had faced the relentless grip of anxiety. Her experiences struck a powerful chord with me, as I could empathize with the way in which anxiety could distort one's perception of reality. She described the sleepless nights, the racing thoughts, and the overwhelming sense of dread that seemed to have no origin or reason. It was as though she had been navigating the same labyrinthine maze of fear and uncertainty that had haunted my own mind.

In our conversations, we discussed the profound impact of anxiety on our daily lives. From the simplest tasks to the most complex challenges, anxiety had a way of permeating every aspect of existence. Yet, as we spoke, I saw in her eyes a glimmer of resilience, a determination to face her anxiety head-on and regain control over her life. Her journey became a testament to the power of the human spirit, an enduring hope that would inspire me on my own path to healing.

Section 2.2: The Colleague's Battle with Depression

One of the most poignant connections I forged was with a colleague who had confronted the profound darkness of depression. His story resonated with me, not in the sense of shared experiences but in the depth of empathy it stirred within me. Listening to his narrative, I was reminded of the haunting abyss that could engulf the mind, leaving a person in a seemingly endless state of despair.

He described the moments when simply getting out of bed felt like an insurmountable task, when even the most routine activities seemed to demand an unbearable effort. I recognized the bleakness of his journey, for I had tasted a similar darkness in my own battle with depression. It was a camaraderie born of the understanding that depression was not a mere emotional state but a relentless force that could eclipse one's very will to live.

Yet, in the midst of his struggle, I discovered a profound reservoir of courage within him. The sheer act of sharing his story was an act of defiance against the grip of depression. He had taken the first step toward healing by speaking openly about his experiences, and in doing so, he had ignited a spark of hope that would become a guiding light for both of us.

Section 2.3: The Neighbour's Intrusive Thoughts

As I continued to connect with those who had faced their own mental battles, I encountered a neighbor whose struggles were marked by intrusive and tormenting thoughts. She described the relentless nature of these thoughts, how they would invade her mind without warning, bringing with them a profound sense of dread and anguish. In her experiences, I saw echoes of the same mental torment that had plagued me for years.

In our conversations, she shared the frustration of trying to explain to others the nature of these thoughts, knowing that they were irrational yet feeling powerless to resist their intrusive presence. It was a shared understanding of the torment that can arise from the inner recesses of one's own mind, a bond that transcended words and required no explanation.

Despite the torment, I found a fierce determination in her, a refusal to be defined by her intrusive thoughts. She had sought help and support, embarking on a journey to regain control over her own mind. Her resilience in the face of such torment was a testament to the indomitable strength that resided within her, and her journey served as a source of inspiration for my own battles.

Section 2.4: The Power of Shared Struggles

In each of these encounters, I discovered the profound power of shared struggles. The stories of my friend with anxiety, my colleague battling depression, and my neighbor with intrusive thoughts became a collective chorus that resonated with my own experiences. It was in their voices that I found solace and understanding, a reminder that I was not alone in the labyrinth of my own mind.

Listening to their narratives, I was struck by the universality of human suffering. These were not isolated battles but a collective testament to the resilience of the human spirit. The realization that others had found the strength to carry on despite their own struggles became a lifeline for me, a source of hope that guided me through even the darkest nights.

In this tapestry of shared experiences, I discovered that we were bound not just by our challenges, but by our collective ability to rise above them. The knowledge that I was not alone in my struggles became a beacon of light, illuminating my path and instilling in me a newfound sense of hope and purpose. As I continued to navigate the labyrinth of my own mind, I was bolstered by the camaraderie and understanding of those who had walked similar paths, and together, we were determined to find our way back to the light.

As I delved deeper into the depths of my own journey and the shared struggles of the remarkable individuals I had connected with, a profound and life-altering sense of purpose began to emerge. This purpose, like the roots of an ancient tree, burrowed into the fertile soil of my soul and took hold, grounding me in a new and transformative way. It was a purpose that was rooted in the very essence of human connection and understanding.

Section 3.1: The Seed of Purpose

The seed of this purpose had been sown in the fertile ground of empathy and shared experiences. I realized that my own battles were not just mine alone, but rather they were a testament to the silent and relentless struggles fought by countless souls across the world. The pain, the uncertainty, and the isolation that had once enveloped me were universal, transcending boundaries of age, gender, and culture.

This realization stirred something profound within me—a longing to bridge the gap that so often separated individuals from the warmth of companionship and the beacon of hope. I had experienced firsthand the desolation of isolation and the despair of facing one's demons alone. Now, I was determined to extend a hand to those who found themselves navigating the labyrinthine corridors of their own minds.

Section 3.2: An Advocate's Journey

With unwavering determination, I made the decision to become an advocate for mental health awareness. My own story, once a closely guarded secret, became a beacon of hope, a testament to the resilience of the human spirit, and a call for understanding and compassion. I recognized that sharing my experiences openly was not a plea for sympathy, but rather a powerful call for empathy. I wanted others to know that they were not alone in their struggles, that there were kindred spirits who understood the weight of their thoughts and the storm within their minds.

My journey as an advocate began in earnest. I utilized online platforms to reach out to those who felt lost and adrift in the labyrinth of their own minds. I shared my story and the battles I had fought with unflinching honesty. It was a vulnerable act, one that laid bare the depths of my pain and my vulnerabilities. But it was an act that resonated with countless individuals who had, until that moment, felt unseen and unheard.

Through the power of the internet, I connected with people from around the world. They reached out to share their own experiences, to confide in someone who understood, even if only from a virtual distance. The connection was palpable, an affirmation that in the realm of shared pain, the barriers of physical distance and anonymity melted away.

Section 3.3: Conversations of Healing

But my mission did not stop with online connections. I felt an immense responsibility to bring the conversation about mental health out from the shadows of the internet and into the tangible world. It was a mission to dispel the stigma and misconceptions that had long cloaked mental health in silence.

I believe that the more we talk openly about these issues, the more we can break down the walls of ignorance and fear. Mental health, I insisted, should be a subject as commonplace as any other. It was a part of the human experience, and it deserved to be understood and accepted as such.

My mission was twofold. I am committed to creating a safe space where individuals could share their deepest fears and struggles without the weight of judgment. I understood the immense courage it can take to bare one's soul, and I want to provide a haven where such vulnerability was met with compassion and support.

In these open dialogues, I saw the transformative power of conversation. Individuals who had long suffered in silence found their voices, and in sharing their stories, they discovered a profound sense of relief. It was as though the very act of speaking out had the ability to lift the burdens of their hearts and minds.

Section 3.4: Kindred Spirits on a Shared Path

As I engaged in these endeavours, I became a bridge between those who suffered in silence and those who were willing to lend an empathetic ear. I witnessed the incredible resilience of the human spirit and the profound transformation that occurred when individuals found themselves in the company of others who had walked similar paths.

In my journey, I met a young woman who had grappled with severe anxiety. Her daily life had been marked by paralysing panic attacks and an unrelenting fear that seemed to hold her captive. She had never spoken openly about her experiences, fearing the judgment and misunderstanding that often-accompanied discussions about mental health.

When she found my story and our subsequent conversations, something remarkable happened. She began to share her own journey, and in doing so, she felt the weight of her isolation begin to lift. It was as though the act of speaking about her anxiety had initiated a process of healing. The burden she had carried for so long was now shared, and the strength of our connection became a source of solace for both of us.

Similarly, I encountered a man whose struggles with depression had left him feeling utterly alone in a world that did not seem to understand. But as he reached out to share his story with me and with others who had faced the same challenges, a transformation occurred. The isolation and despair he had once known were replaced with the warmth of camaraderie and the promise of hope. The collective strength of kindred spirits on a shared path became a source of inspiration for all involved.

Section 3.5: The Tapestry of Empathy

In the world of mental health advocacy, I realized that every individual's journey was a unique thread in a vast and interconnected tapestry of empathy. Each story, each struggle, and each triumph contributed to this beautiful mosaic of understanding and compassion.

The conversations and connections that had once been a solitary whisper of despair were now a collective roar of resilience and hope. The stigma that had shrouded mental health was slowly but steadily eroding as more and more individuals shared their experiences and found solace in the company of kindred spirits.

I often reflected on the immense power of human connection and the potential for transformation that lay within it. The isolated souls I had met were no longer alone in the darkness of their minds. They had become part of a community that celebrated their strengths and offered support in their moments of vulnerability.

I felt a profound sense of gratitude. Gratitude for the opportunity to connect with remarkable individuals who had shown me the boundless strength of the human spirit. Gratitude for the chance to be a bridge between those who had suffered in silence and those who were willing to listen with open hearts. And gratitude for the privilege of witnessing the transformative power of shared experiences and the profound healing that could emerge from the simple act of speaking one's truth.

I often thought about the young sailor I had been during my time in the Navy, battling my own demons in silence. If I would have known then what I know now, that there were people who understood the weight of my thoughts and the storm within my mind, perhaps my journey toward healing would have begun sooner.

I realized that I had become a beacon of hope for others who were navigating the unseen labyrinth of their own minds. I had become a testament to the power of resilience, the importance of empathy, and the transformative potential of shared experiences.

Section 3.6: A Journey of Healing and Connection

My journey had evolved from one of isolation and despair to one of healing and connection. I had found my purpose in advocating for mental health awareness and in reaching out to those who felt lost in the depths of their own struggles.

As I continued to connect with remarkable individuals from all walks of life, I marvelled at the richness of the human experience. We were bound not just by our shared challenges, but by our collective strength and resilience. The walls of stigma and misunderstanding that had long surrounded mental health were slowly but steadily crumbling, replaced by a tapestry of empathy and compassion.

Through the power of conversation and the strength of connection, we were changing the narrative about mental health. We were creating a world where individuals felt safe to share their fears, their vulnerabilities, and their triumphs. We were fostering an environment where the isolation of mental health struggles could be replaced by the warmth of understanding and companionship.

Section 3.7: A Shared Path Forward

The conversation about mental health was not just a matter of speaking openly; it was a matter of listening and empathizing. It was a matter of offering support and understanding to those who needed it the most.

As I looked toward the future, I saw a world where mental

health was understood, accepted, and embraced. I saw a world where individuals did not have to suffer in silence, where they could share their stories and find solace in the company of kindred spirits. It was a world where empathy was the cornerstone of understanding, and where the invisible battles of the mind were met with compassion and support.

In the ever-evolving course of empathy and connection, I saw a shared path forward. It was a path that led us away from the isolation of mental health struggles and toward a future where the warmth of human understanding illuminated the way. It was a journey that would continue to evolve, but it was a journey I was committed to.

Section 3.8: A Beacon of Hope for the Future

My advocacy work has become not just a purpose, but a calling—a calling to be a beacon of hope for those who were navigating the tumultuous waters of mental health. I had learned that the journey toward healing was not one that could be taken in isolation. It was a journey that required the strength and understanding of a community that extended its hand to those in need.

As I looked back on my own battles with mental health, I saw the incredible transformation that had occurred when I reached out to others and when others reached out to me. The isolation and despair I had once known were replaced by a sense of belonging and understanding. It was a transformation that had given me a renewed sense of purpose and a profound sense of gratitude.

In the tapestry of empathy and connection, I found solace and strength. I found a community of individuals who had faced their own demons and emerged as beacons of hope. And I found a world that was slowly but surely changing its perception of mental health, one conversation at a time.

In my advocacy journey, I had discovered that there was a profound beauty in vulnerability and a strength in shared struggles. I had learned that the power of empathy could bridge the gaps that separated individuals from the understanding and support they so desperately needed.

As I looked to the future, I saw a world where mental health was not a interdiction subject, but a topic that was met with open hearts and open minds. I saw a world where individuals were not defined by their struggles, but by their resilience and their capacity to connect with others.

And so, with a heart full of courage and a spirit unyielding, I continued to traverse the path of advocacy and connection. I knew that the journey was ongoing, but it was a journey that held the promise of a brighter and more compassionate future for all.

Section 4: A Radiant of Light

In the eyes of my daughter and stepson, I saw the reflection of my own vulnerability. They, too, are facing the challenges of growing up in a world that often misunderstood mental health. It has become my responsibility to be a **radiant** of light for them, to show them that their struggles did not define them. Together, we **will** embrace the difficult conversations, discussing emotions and fears openly.

My home became a sanctuary where mental health was not a foreign subject but a natural topic of discussion. We shared stories of courage, of battles won and lost, and in doing so, we strengthened the bonds of our family. It was my hope that by nurturing their emotional intelligence, I could empower them to face life's challenges with resilience and self-compassion.

As I continued my advocacy work, I witnessed the transformative power of shared story's Strangers became allies, bound by the understanding that mental health was a shared human experience. Together, we challenged the stigma that shrouded mental illness, replacing ignorance with empathy.

In the quiet moments of reflection, I realized that my journey was not just a personal odyssey but a collective endeavour. It was a story of triumph over adversity, a testament to the strength of the human spirit. Through my words and actions, I hoped to inspire others to embrace their own stories, to recognize the beauty in their resilience, and to know that they, too, were never truly alone.

And so, in the depths of my reflection, I found not just the answers to my own questions but a purpose that transcended my individual struggles. My mission was clear—to be a voice for the voiceless, to shine a light on the shadows of the mind, and to remind the world that amidst the darkness, there existed the possibility of hope, connection, and understanding.

Chapter 5: Therapy or Torture: Navigating the Trauma of Seeking Help

In the hushed corridors of the military hospital, I found myself face-to-face with a psychiatrist—a person meant to help me, to guide me through the labyrinth of my thoughts. Little did I know that this encounter would leave me scarred, my trust in the healing power of therapy shattered.

Section 1: The Broken Promise of Help

During my time in the navy, seeking therapy was not a choice but an order. The weight of my struggles had become too heavy to bear alone, and the military, in its stern wisdom, had decided that therapy was the solution. With a flicker of hope, I walked into the psychiatrist's office, believing that finally, I would find the understanding and support I desperately needed.

Instead, what I encountered was a barrage of judgment and dismissiveness. The psychiatrist's words cut through me like shards of glass. "Life's hard," they said, as if the complexities of my mind could be reduced to a mere cliché. "Snap out of it," they declared, as if my struggles were a mere figment of imagination. In that moment, therapy transformed into torture, a cruel reminder that seeking help could sometimes lead to further trauma.

Section 2: The Reluctant Decision

The experience with the military psychiatrist left me deeply scarred. I became reluctant to seek help through traditional channels. The very thought of opening up to a doctor, of exposing my vulnerabilities only to face judgment and callousness, filled me with dread. The scars of that encounter became a barrier, one that kept me from the very help I needed.

But amidst my reluctance, a spark of resilience flickered within me. I refused to let one bad experience define my journey toward healing. Instead of relying on professionals, I turned inward, embracing the power of self-reflection and writing. It was through the written word that I found solace, a means to express the turmoil within me without the fear of judgment.

Section 3: Turning Pain into Purpose

In the depths of my despair, I discovered a purpose that transcended my own struggles. I realized that my painful experience was not unique—that there were others like me, individuals who had faced the harsh reality of inadequate mental health support. It was this realization that fueled my determination to share my story, to be a voice for those who had been silenced by the very system meant to help them.

Through writing, I found catharsis. Each word penned on the page became a release, a way to unburden my soul. But more than that, it became a lifeline for others who resonated with my experiences. As my words found their way into the hearts of readers, I witnessed a collective sigh of relief—a recognition that they were not alone in their struggles, that there was someone out there who understood their pain.

Section 4: The Healing Power of Shared Stories

In sharing my own journey, I began to collect stories from others who had faced similar challenges. Their experiences echoed mine, painting a vivid picture of a broken system that failed to provide the support and understanding so desperately needed. These shared stories became a chorus of voices, a rallying cry for change.

I realized that my writing had become a form of therapy— not just for me but for countless others who found solace in the resonance of shared experiences. Together, we forged a community, a safe haven where judgment had no place, and compassion and understanding were the pillars upon which we leaned.

Section 5: A New Path to Healing

In the absence of traditional therapy, I discovered an unconventional path to healing—one that involved the power of community and the strength of the written word. Through writing, I found a way to navigate the intricate corridors of my mind, unravelling the knots of trauma and pain. Through sharing, I found validation and empathy, two essential elements that had been missing from my earlier therapeutic encounters.

As I embraced this new path, I realized that healing was not a linear journey but a mosaic of experiences. Each setback and triumph became a part of the intricate tapestry of my recovery. And in the process, I found a sense of purpose that went beyond my own struggles. I became an advocate for change, a voice that challenged the status quo and demanded a more compassionate approach to mental health support.

In the face of my own painful past, I had found a way to transform trauma into resilience and isolation into community. The scars remained, but they no longer defined me. Instead, they became a testament to my strength and a reminder of the power of the human spirit to endure, to overcome, and to rise above the challenges that life will bring.

And so, with each word I wrote, with each story I shared, I became a beacon of hope for those who had lost faith in the healing power of therapy. My journey, once marred by a painful encounter, had become a testament to the resilience of the human spirit and the transformative power of sharing our deepest pains and vulnerabilities.

In the chapters of my life, therapy had indeed been a form of torture, but through writing and community, I had discovered a new path to healing—one that embraced empathy, understanding, and the unwavering belief that no one should ever have to face their battles alone.

Chapter 6: Resilience Beyond the Shadows

In the quiet depths of my soul, I confronted the demons that had once held me captive. Depression, with its heavy cloak of despair, and anxiety, with its relentless grip on my thoughts, were no longer adversaries to fear. Instead, they became challenges I was determined to overcome. Each day, as I woke up to the world, I faced the shadows within me with a newfound courage. I embraced therapy, self-reflection, and the unwavering support of my loved ones as my weapons against the darkness. With every small victory, I felt the weight of the chains around me loosen, empowering me to take another step forward.

In the laughter of my daughter and the warmth of my partner's touch, I discovered the strength to persevere. My family became my sanctuary—a place where love and understanding flowed freely. Their unwavering support was a balm to my wounded soul, a reminder that I was not alone in my battle. It was their belief in me, their unwavering faith that I could overcome, that fueled my determination. I refused to let my struggles eclipse the happiness and security I could provide for them. Their smiles became my motivation, lighting the path ahead with hope and determination.

Every day was a triumph, a victory over the darkness that threatened to consume me. I woke up with a newfound sense of purpose, ready to face the challenges that rest ahead. The mere act of getting out of bed became a testament to my strength. I no longer viewed my struggles as insurmountable obstacles but as opportunities for growth and resilience. Each day became a canvas, and I painted it with colours of determination, hope, and unwavering resolve. I celebrated not just the big milestones but also the small victories—a genuine smile, a moment of peace, a day without overwhelming despair. Each of these moments reinforced my belief in my own strength and reminded me that I was capable of weathering any storm.

I refused to be a victim of my circumstances; instead, I chose to be a survivor. I fought not just for myself but for the countless others who felt the weight of mental illness pressing down on them. My struggle was no longer just mine; it was a shared battle, a collective fight against the stigma and ignorance that surrounded mental health. Every step I took was a step toward a brighter tomorrow, not just for me but for everyone who had ever felt the crushing weight of despair.

I made a conscious decision to embrace life, one moment at a time. I learned to savour the simple pleasures—the taste of a warm cup of coffee, the gentle touch of the wind on my skin, the sound of my children's laughter filling the room. In these moments, I found solace and gratitude. I realized that life, with all its challenges, was still a gift, a precious opportunity to experience joy, love, and connection. Instead of dwelling on the past or worrying about an uncertain future, I chose to be present. I embraced mindfulness, allowing myself to fully engage with each moment, no matter how fleeting. It was in these moments of presence that I found peace, a respite from the storms within my mind. Each moment became a reminder that life, despite its hardships, was still worth living.

In the depths of my struggle, I made a promise—a solemn vow to myself and to every soul battling similar demons. I pledged to be a beacon of hope, a living testament to the fact that even in the face of adversity, one could emerge stronger and more resilient. My journey, once marred by pain, had transformed into a source of inspiration for others walking similar paths. I carried the torch of hope, illuminating the path for those lost in the darkness of mental illness. I became an advocate, a voice that challenged the status quo and demanded a more compassionate approach to mental health support. I stand tall, ready to face whatever challenges lay ahead, confident in my ability to conquer the darkness and emerge stronger on the other side.

And so, with every sunrise, I reaffirmed my commitment to life, love, and the pursuit of happiness. My mental illness would not define me; instead, it would serve as a reminder of the battles I had fought and the victories I had achieved. I was more than my struggles—I was a survivor, a warrior, and a living testament to the power of resilience and unwavering determination. With each passing day, I continued to fight, not just for my own sake but for the countless individuals who felt the weight of mental illness pressing down on them. I refused to let depression and anxiety rob me of the love, laughter, and beauty life had to offer. Instead, I chose to embrace every moment, to be present for my family, and to face each day with unyielding determination. In the battle against my own mind, I discovered an inner strength I never knew I possessed. And as I moved forward, I did so with the knowledge that my struggles were not a sign of weakness but a testament to my resilience. I stand tall, ready to face whatever challenges lay ahead, confident in my ability to conquer the darkness and emerge stronger on the other side. And so, with every sunrise, I reaffirmed my commitment to life, love, and the pursuit of happiness. My mental illness would not define me; instead, it would serve as a reminder of the battles I had fought and the victories I had achieved. I was more than my struggles—I was a survivor, a warrior, and a living testament to the power of resilience and unwavering determination.

Amidst the battles, one truth shone through the darkness: I had not been the father figure my son deserved. The pain of this realization cut deep, becoming a driving force for change. I made a solemn pledge to be a better step-dad, to offer him the love and guidance he needed and deserved. No longer would I let my struggles overshadow his need for stability and care. I vowed to be there for him, to listen, to understand, and to support him in every possible way. He deserved a strong role model, someone he could look up to with pride, and I was determined to become that person.

For my daughter, I pledged to be the unwavering rock she could always rely on. Life's journey was bound to be tumultuous, marked by heartbreaks and challenges. I promised to stand by her side through every breakup, every setback, and every triumph. My love for her knew no bounds, and I would be her constant, her anchor in the stormy sea of life. No obstacle would be insurmountable with her father's unwavering support.

From ballet recitals to baseball games, I am committed to being their biggest cheerleader. Regardless of my struggles, I would be in the stands, clapping the loudest, and shouting their names with pride. Their dreams would be mine, and I would do everything in my power to nurture their passions and aspirations. Through the highs and lows, victories and defeats, I would be there, teaching them that perseverance and determination were the keys to success.

In these commitments, I found a renewed sense of purpose. My family became my driving force, propelling me forward with a strength I hadn't known before. The battles against my mental illness had not diminished my capacity to love and care; if anything, they had amplified it. And so, with unwavering determination, I faced the future, ready to be the father my children deserved, the partner my significant other needed, and a beacon of hope for all those navigating the stormy seas of mental health challenges.

In the chapters of my life, I rewrote the narrative. I was not just a survivor; I was a dedicated father, a loving partner, and a resilient soul who refused to be defined by his struggles. My journey toward resilience became an inspiration not just for me but for those around me. And with every step I took, I carried the weight of my past battles but also the promise of a brighter, more hopeful future.

Chapter 7: Embracing the Journey

In the tapestry of life, there are threads of joy and sorrow, woven together to create a unique and intricate pattern. As I moved forward on my journey, I embraced the unpredictability of life, understanding that both challenges and triumphs were essential elements of the human experience. Chapter 7 marked a new beginning, a chapter where I confronted my fears, celebrated my victories, and learned profound lessons about resilience, love, and self-acceptance.

As I faced the challenges of each day, I confronted the lingering shadows of my past. The scars of my battles were reminders of my strength, but they were also testament to the battles I had fought. Therapy sessions became not just a means of healing but a path to self-discovery. I delved into the roots of my struggles, unearthing buried emotions and confronting long-buried traumas. Each session was a step toward understanding myself better, peeling away the layers of pain to reveal the resilient spirit beneath.

In sharing my story, I became a beacon of hope for others. I found solace in the knowledge that my words resonated with those who had walked similar paths. Through support groups and advocacy work, I connected with individuals who, like me, had battled the demons of mental illness. Together, we formed a community—a family bound not by blood but by shared experiences. I offered a listening ear, a comforting presence, and a message of hope to those still navigating the labyrinth of mental health challenges. In helping others, I found a renewed sense of purpose, a calling to be the light in someone else's darkness.

Amidst the chaos of my mind, I discovered the transformative power of self-compassion. I learned to embrace my flaws and imperfections, understanding that they were not weaknesses but facets of my humanity. Through mindfulness practices and self-reflection, I cultivated a kinder relationship with myself. Instead of berating myself for my struggles, I extended the same empathy and understanding I offered to others. Self-compassion became my anchor, grounding me in moments of self-doubt and despair.

In the tapestry of my life, relationships played a central role. I nurtured the bonds with my family, cherishing every moment spent with my partner, children, and loved ones. I learned to communicate my feelings, fears, and dreams openly, fostering a deeper understanding between us. As I supported my children through their journeys, I discovered the immense joy that came from witnessing their growth and accomplishments. Love became the guiding force in my life, transcending the boundaries of my struggles and offering a profound sense of belonging.

In the relentless pursuit of perfection, I had traversed a path fraught with frustration and disappointment. I had long believed that the peak of existence was marked by flawlessness, by the ability to orchestrate every facet of life to symphonic precision. Yet, despite my tireless efforts and unwavering dedication, the pursuit of perfection was akin to chasing a mirage in the desert, shimmering tantalizingly in the distance but forever elusive.

It was a journey marked by sleepless nights and endless self-critique. The unrelenting pressure to attain perfection seeped into every corner of my life, casting an unforgiving light on every flaw, every imperfection, and every moment of vulnerability. My self-worth became inextricably tied to the ceaseless quest for flawlessness, and my identity was subsumed by an insatiable desire to achieve the unattainable.

Then, one day, in the midst of yet another relentless endeavor to mold my existence into a perfect tableau, I stumbled upon a revelation. It was an epiphany that shook the very foundations of my belief system and shook me to my core. It was the dawning realization that life's richness lay not in the sterile perfection I had so fervently pursued, but in the raw, unfiltered, and gloriously imperfect moments that painted the tapestry of existence.

In that moment, I decided to step off the relentless treadmill of perfection and instead chose to embrace my imperfections. I discovered a profound beauty in the authenticity of these messy, unscripted moments. Each scrape, each dent, and each scar that life had etched upon me were not blemishes but testaments to resilience. They were the very things that made me who I was, each one telling a story of survival, adaptation, and growth.

Embracing my imperfections was not an easy journey. It was a process of unlearning, of undoing the conditioning that had led me to believe that perfect equated to valuable. But in the midst of this transformation, I found a sense of liberation, a newfound freedom that allowed me to breathe more deeply, to laugh more freely, and to take life less seriously.

I began to celebrate my ability to rise after each fall, to dust myself off, and to keep moving forward. It was a conscious shift in perspective, viewing these moments of vulnerability as stepping-stones rather than stumbling blocks. They became not the symbols of failure, but rather the milestones of growth and development. I learned to acknowledge my imperfections not as limitations but as opportunities, opportunities to learn, to adapt, and to become a more resilient version of myself.

In this newfound outlook, imperfection transformed into a source of resilience. It was a reminder that it was okay to stumble and falter as long as I continued to move forward. Life was no longer an unending race towards perfection, but a journey filled with twists, turns, and detours. Each challenge, each setback, became a chance to learn, to adjust, and to evolve. I began to see imperfections as the threads that wove the rich tapestry of my life, creating a multi-dimensional picture that was far more beautiful and meaningful than any glossy, airbrushed image of perfection.

It was through this transformation that I uncovered the profound beauty of embracing imperfection, a beauty that resided not only in the self-acceptance of my own shortcomings but in the acceptance of others as well. I began to understand that every person, no matter how polished their exterior might appear, carried their own set of imperfections and vulnerabilities.

This newfound perspective allowed me to forge deeper, more authentic connections with those around me. I realized that we were all imperfect beings navigating the complex terrain of life, and it was in our shared vulnerabilities that true bonds of empathy and understanding could be formed. I no longer saw flaws in others as weaknesses, but as badges of courage, testimonies to their own battles and triumphs. This shift in perception enriched my relationships, making them more genuine, more empathetic, and more profound.

My journey from the relentless pursuit of perfection to the embrace of imperfection was not without its challenges. There were moments of doubt and self-judgment, moments when the siren song of perfectionism called me back to its familiar, but ultimately unfulfilling, shores. However, I had tasted the richness of life's imperfections, and I could not go back to the empty promise of an unattainable ideal.

As time passed, my life transformed in remarkable ways. I became more resilient in the face of adversity, more compassionate in my interactions with others, and more at peace with myself. The world took on a different hue, one that was vibrant, textured, and profoundly beautiful in its imperfections. I found joy in the simple moments, the laughter that emerged from unexpected mishaps, and the wisdom that bloomed from navigating challenges. Each day became a canvas, and I was the artist, painting my existence with the colors of authenticity and self-acceptance. Imperfection was no longer something to be feared or avoided; it was the very essence of life, the heartbeat that pulsed through the complex, messy, and utterly wondrous symphony of existence.

In the end, the pursuit of perfection had led me to a profound realization. It was the acceptance of imperfection that had unveiled the true beauty of life, the beauty that resided in its unscripted, messy, and wonderfully imperfect moments. It was a transformation that had set me free, allowing me to live more fully, to love more deeply, and to appreciate the exquisite imperfection that made each day a masterpiece in its own, right.

Chapter 7 was not a conclusion but a continuation—a journey of ongoing growth and self-discovery. With each day, I embraced the opportunity to learn, evolve, and become a better version of myself. I faced the future with a newfound sense of optimism, understanding that my past struggles had shaped me but did not define me. I carried the lessons of resilience, love, and self-acceptance with me, using them as stepping-stones toward a brighter tomorrow.

In the pages of Chapter 7, I discovered the strength to confront my fears, the courage to share my story, and the wisdom to accept myself fully. The journey was far from over, but I embraced it with open arms, ready to navigate the twists and turns that lay ahead. As I closed this chapter, I did so with a heart full of gratitude—for the lessons learned, the battles fought, and the unwavering support that had carried me through. The next chapter awaited, and I faced it with hope, determination, and a newfound appreciation for the beauty of life's complexities.

Chapter 8: Embracing New Horizons

Chapter 8 of my life unfolded as a vibrant, dynamic thread, weaving its way through the fabric of my existence. This chapter marked a period of profound transformation and renewal.

Change, an ever-present force in the tapestry of life, was no longer a source of trepidation for me. Instead, I wholeheartedly embraced it, recognizing the profound opportunities it brought. Like a mariner navigating a ship through turbulent waters, I steered through the winds of change with grace and determination. I understood that each twist and turn presented a chance for personal growth.

Life's ever-changing currents became my playground, and I learned to dance upon their waves. I stood tall amidst the unpredictable gusts, with roots growing deeper into the fertile soil of possibility. The winds of change carried whispers of new beginnings and unexplored territories.

Embracing change had become an art I had crafted over the years. Life's uncertainties no longer sent shivers down my spine; they invigorated me. Challenges represented adventures waiting to unfold, sculptors shaping my character, and horizons extending beyond the limits of my imagination.

With an open heart, I viewed each day as a promise of new opportunities for self-discovery and growth. Fear of the unknown was replaced by exhilaration. Within the boundless embrace of change, I found life's essence—a relentless and awe-inspiring evolution that allowed me to unfold, just like the universe itself did.

In the pursuit of passion, I embarked on a profound journey, unearthing the essence of my being. Creativity became my sanctuary, offering solace and an outlet for my soul's exploration. Through writing, painting, or music, I traveled to artistic realms where I roamed free, unburdened by life's constraints. Here, I was both the explorer and the creator, shaping worlds, painting emotions, and composing notes from my heart.

Advocacy work emerged as a calling, resonating deeply with my core. It became my mission, allowing me to be a voice for the voiceless and a champion for the marginalized. I dedicated my time, energy, and heart to causes that kindled the flames of compassion. Through my work, I aimed to create ripples of change that extended beyond my own existence.

Hobbies, once casual diversions, transformed into profound sources of joy. They became instrumental in self-discovery and wellsprings of happiness. These pursuits painted my days with vibrant colors of enthusiasm and creativity. Each contributed a unique hue and texture to the grand design of my life's story.

In my passions and advocacies, I found a profound sense of purpose. They became the pillars upon which I built the structure of my identity, shaping the way I viewed the world. In creativity and purpose-driven endeavors, I discovered the truest expression of who I was and aspired to be.

Gratitude became a practice deeply woven into my life. It allowed me to find wonder in life's simple moments, seeing challenges as opportunities in disguise and setbacks as valuable lessons. Gratitude was my sanctuary, offering solace even during life's fiercest turbulence. It revealed hidden jewels adorning my journey.

Vulnerability, once concealed beneath layers of self-preservation, emerged as my most potent and authentic strength. I shed protective armor to reveal my innermost self to the world, becoming a beacon of hope for those in similar struggles. Sharing my journey created connections that were deep and authentic, forging bridges of understanding and acceptance.

Balance, the equilibrium between chaos and tranquility, underpinned my existence. I listened to the whispers of my body, mind, and spirit, nurturing their needs and limitations. Self-care became a sacred ritual, nurturing my well-being with unwavering devotion. In solitude, I rekindled my connection with my essence, embarking on a profound inner journey.

Balance taught me to harmonize the chaos and tranquility within and around me. It was the symphony of my existence, where life's challenges were met with self-care, solitude, and resilience. It illuminated the path to a well-lived life, appreciated for its harmonious dance between discord and serenity.

Empowered by my resilience, I became a torchbearer of hope in a world sometimes shrouded in darkness. I reached out to those adrift in despair, guiding them toward the light. Advocacy and courageous conversations became my mission, tearing down the barriers of mental health stigma. I worked tirelessly to provide support, understanding, and solace for those grappling with their mental well-being.

My journey had evolved into a mission that transcended my personal experience. It was a testament to the resilience of the human spirit and the boundless capacity for compassion within us all. Through this mission, I discovered that there was no greater reward than knowing I had been instrumental in helping others find their way from despair to hope and healing. Chapter 8 was a testament to my enduring spirit, where I embraced life's complexities with grace. I understood that the chapters yet to come held endless possibilities. With every step, I welcomed the adventures that lay ahead. I embarked on the next chapter with unwavering courage, eager to embrace new horizons.

Bonus Section: Supporting Your Spouse Through Mental Health Struggles

In the quiet, intimate corridors of a relationship, mental health struggles can cast a long and lingering shadow. It's not just the individual who grapples with the tempest within; their partner, their confidant, their lover, is also thrust into tumultuous waters. Being the spouse of someone navigating the intricate labyrinth of mental health challenges can be a journey filled with emotional turbulence, bewilderment, and, at times, a profound sense of isolation. In these moments of profound darkness, when words often feel inadequate, it is paramount to find ways to support your spouse. Here, we delve deep into the intricate nuances of this shared voyage, exploring the myriad challenges faced by spouses and providing tangible strategies to help navigate the complex terrain of mental health together.

Section 1: Understanding the Invisible Battles

In the labyrinth of a relationship where mental health battles remain hidden beneath the surface, these struggles often go unnoticed, disguised behind everyday smiles and the monotony of daily life. For spouses, deciphering these subtle signs can be akin to solving a complex, enigmatic puzzle. Your partner, the person with whom you've shared your life and your love, might begin to exhibit gradual changes that, at first glance, seem elusive. Their laughter, once a familiar and comforting melody, might gradually lose its familiar tune, fading like the echoes of a distant memory. The gleam in their eyes, once vibrant and vivacious, may flicker like a fragile candle flame in a gentle breeze. The isolation they wrestle with can become almost palpable, casting a heavy presence, an unspoken burden, within the confines of your shared space. As a spouse, it is not merely important but crucial to discern these distinctions, to be attuned not only to the words they speak but also to the poignant silences that linger between you.

In the intricate fabric of a partnership darkened by the clouds of mental health struggles, silence takes on a profound significance. Each pause becomes a note in the symphony of your shared existence. Your partner might begin to withdraw, stepping back into this silence, and in doing so, leaving you, their confidant, feeling like a solitary observer on the outskirts of their world. It's in these moments that your presence can speak volumes. Sitting with them in the quiet, extending a hand to hold or a shoulder to lean on, can serve as a bridge across the chasm that their silence creates. It's essential to understand that their silence is not a rejection of your presence, but rather an unspoken invitation, a subtle plea for you to share in the weight of their thoughts and emotions. In this intricate dance of silence and connection, you'll discover that the absence of words does not signify a lack of communication. Instead, it's an opportunity to connect on a deeper, more profound level, where the quietude itself becomes a language of understanding.

In the domain of mental health struggles, emotions run deep, like underground rivers that ebb and flow. Your spouse may find themselves oscillating between hope and despair, their emotional landscape resembling a rollercoaster ride. At times, these emotions may plummet into the depths of profound sadness, while at other moments, they may experience fleeting glimpses of joy.

Your role is to be the anchor in the storm, the unwavering presence that provides solace during turbulent times. This means offering reassurance that even in their darkest moments, you stand resolutely by their side, a steadfast pillar of support. In this emotional journey, empathy and understanding are your most potent allies, providing a lifeline for your loved one as they navigate the complex terrain of their inner world.

Mental health challenges are often rooted in deep-seated vulnerabilities. Your spouse may find it difficult to articulate their deepest fears, their self-doubts, or the traumas that may haunt their past. Creating a safe haven where vulnerability is not only tolerated but wholeheartedly embraced is of immeasurable value. Encourage open and honest conversations where the unfiltered truth can flow freely, devoid of judgment or reproach. Your willingness to listen without attempting to 'fix' everything serves as a profound source of solace. In these moments, your acceptance of their vulnerability provides the foundation upon which they can build their path to healing and recovery.

Section 2: The Weight of Silence

Amidst the labyrinthine journey of confronting their mental health challenges, there will be times when your spouse, like an introverted hermit, seeks refuge in the cocoon of silence. In these moments, you may find yourself relegated to the periphery of their world, the cold winds of isolation brushing against your heart. It's here, within the profound stillness that envelopes their troubled psyche, that your presence takes on an unspoken significance, like a message conveyed without words. This is where the eloquence of companionship comes into play.

In the narrative of a relationship, the unspoken is often as powerful as the spoken. Silence, especially in the face of mental health struggles, is not the absence of communication; rather, it's a distinct form of conversation. It's in the moments when your spouse remains cocooned in their private world, their lips sealed and words left unspoken, that you can become a master interpreter of their emotions. In these wordless conversations, your presence is your most eloquent language.

Silence, when embraced, is not a fortress but a bridge. It's a subtle invitation that your spouse extends to you. It's a hand reaching out in the darkness, hoping for a touch, a silent plea for understanding. When they retreat into their cocoon of quietude, they are not pushing you away; instead, they are beckoning you to share the weight of their thoughts and emotions. In this unspoken invitation lies the opportunity for you to build a deeper connection, to journey through their struggles together, with the power of your presence as a beacon in their silent sanctuary.

Section 3: Navigating the Labyrinth of Emotions

In the complex and turbulent domain of mental health struggles, emotions run deep and wide, like untamed rivers flowing through the landscape of your spouse's inner world. As their partner, you find yourself on an emotional odyssey, journeying through the peaks and valleys of their feelings. There will be moments when hope blossoms like a delicate flower, only to be overshadowed by the looming clouds of despair. Profound sadness may cast a long shadow, yet brief and elusive moments of joy still manage to pierce through the darkness. It's a rollercoaster ride, one that you have no choice but to embark upon.

The emotional landscape of mental health struggles is akin to a kaleidoscope, a mesmerizing but unpredictable symphony of feelings. In the realm of this ever-changing emotional terrain, your spouse may find themselves engulfed by waves of intense sadness, only to be followed by the gentle breezes of momentary happiness. As their partner, you occupy a seat beside them on this emotional rollercoaster, the harness of your presence securing you both in the ride.

In the tempestuous seas of emotional upheaval, your steadfast presence becomes the anchor that keeps your spouse's ship from being swept away by the storm. Even when their emotions reach their darkest depths, your unwavering support is a lighthouse guiding them safely through the night. It's in these tumultuous moments that you have the chance to be their rock, offering not just a safe harbor but a reassuring beacon. You reassure them that no matter how turbulent the emotional seas may become, you are there beside them, unyielding, strong, and a source of solace.

Section 4: Embracing Vulnerability

The genesis of mental health battles often resides in the realm of deeply rooted vulnerabilities, buried like fragile seeds in the soil of your spouse's psyche. It's in these vulnerabilities where the roots of their struggles firmly entrench themselves. Fears, self-doubts, and the haunting specters of past traumas lurk in the shadows, shaping the contours of their emotional landscape. The ability to acknowledge and navigate these vulnerabilities is a vital aspect of their journey towards healing.

In the world of mental health struggles, vulnerability becomes the cornerstone of recovery. Your spouse may find it challenging to articulate their deepest fears and insecurities, their silent battles that have raged within them. To create a safe haven where vulnerability is not merely accepted but cherished is a priceless gift. It's a space where your partner can strip away the armor of their defenses and expose their raw, authentic selves without fear of judgment or reproach.

Embracing vulnerability requires the delicate art of unburdening. Your partner may carry a heavy load, and the willingness to share their innermost thoughts can be an act of profound release. In this space, your role transforms into that of an empathetic listener, a companion who is there not to 'fix' everything but to provide a sanctuary where honesty flows freely. It's in these unguarded moments, devoid of judgment, where your willingness to listen, to hold space for their pain and their truth, becomes a profound source of solace and connection.

Section 5: The Art of Patience and Perseverance

In the intricate tapestry of mental health, healing does not follow a linear path. It's not a straightforward journey from illness to recovery, but rather a convoluted mosaic of progress and setbacks, of triumphant moments and challenging trials. As a spouse navigating this complex terrain alongside your partner, you are confronted with the unpredictable nature of their healing journey. There will be days when the sun shines brightly, and the path ahead seems to be clear and welcoming. Your partner may exhibit signs of improvement, and it can feel like the darkness is retreating. However, there will also be days when the skies turn overcast, and the struggles seem insurmountable. On these darker days, your partner may retreat into the abyss of their mental health issues, and it's during these moments that your unwavering support becomes the guiding light in their tumultuous journey.

As a spouse, your role in this journey of mental health is unlike any other. Your patience takes on a unique quality, one that transcends the boundaries of ordinary waiting. It's-a-patience like no other because it's interwoven with profound love and unwavering commitment. You understand that your partner's healing does not adhere to a set schedule or a linear progression. It unfolds at its own pace, dictated by the ebb and flow of their inner battles. Your patience becomes a beacon of hope in the turbulent seas of mental health, a source of strength and reassurance. It's the steady heartbeat that resounds in the darkest of nights, a reminder that you are there, anchored by your love and dedication. In the labyrinth of mental health, setbacks are not uncommon. They can manifest as sudden relapses, unexpected episodes of distress, or moments when your partner feels overwhelmed by their struggles. These are the times when the darkness seems to close in, and the path forward becomes shrouded in uncertainty. As a spouse, witnessing these setbacks can be heart-wrenching. It's during these moments that your patience and unwavering support shine the brightest. You become a steadfast presence amid the storm, offering solace and understanding when it is needed most. Your ability to persevere through these challenging times is a testament to the depth of your love and commitment.

The journey of mental health is often portrayed as a path from illness to recovery, but it's important to recognize that for many, it's a journey without a defined endpoint. The road may be long and winding, marked by both progress and setbacks. There may be no final destination where your partner is entirely free from their mental health challenges. It's in acknowledging this endless horizon that your unwavering support becomes even more significant. Your steadfastness is not dependent on reaching a specific goal; it's a commitment to being there, regardless of the path your partner's healing journey takes. Your love and patience become a powerful force, providing a sense of security and assurance as you both navigate the complexities of mental health.

The journey of mental health, with its twists and turns, challenges and triumphs, is woven into the tapestry of your love. Your unwavering support and enduring patience are the threads that bind this intricate tapestry together. They are the foundation upon which your love is built, a love that transcends the boundaries of mental health struggles. Your commitment is a testament to the depth of your love, a love that endures through the darkest nights and the most challenging days. It's a love that says, "I am here, no matter what," and it becomes a source of strength, hope, and resilience in the face of mental health challenges.

Section 6: Encouraging Professional Help

In the labyrinth of mental health, there are junctures where the support of loved ones, no matter how unwavering, reaches its limits. It's during these moments that the intervention of a professional becomes not just a choice but a necessity. Encouraging your spouse to embark on the path of therapy or counseling is an act steeped in profound love and care. It signifies a recognition of the complexity of mental health struggles and the need for specialized guidance. It is not, by any means, an admission of failure or weakness, but rather a courageous and forward-looking step toward healing and well-being.

While the importance of professional intervention is undeniable, it is essential to acknowledge the challenges and stigma often associated with seeking therapy or counseling. The fear of judgment, the misconceptions surrounding mental health, and the weight of societal expectations can cast a long shadow on the decision to reach out for professional help. As a spouse, you play a crucial role in dispelling these stigmas and providing a supportive environment for your partner to take this vital step. It is a journey of education, empathy, and the eradication of unfounded taboos.

The decision to seek professional help for mental health challenges is an act of profound courage. It's a testament to your spouse's inner strength and resilience. Acknowledge and celebrate this courage. It's a milestone on their journey toward healing and well-being. It's an affirmation of their commitment to navigate the complexities of their mental health and find the support they need. As a spouse, your role is that of a cheerleader, a steadfast advocate who stands by their side and applauds their bravery.

Supporting your spouse through the process of seeking professional help requires a deep well of empathy. It's a time when your ability to understand and share in their feelings becomes a priceless asset. Your partner may experience a whirlwind of emotions—apprehension, hope, relief, and uncertainty. Being there to listen, to validate their feelings, and to offer reassurance can be a tremendous source of comfort. Your empathy becomes a bridge between their emotions and the professional support they are about to receive.

CONCLUSION

As I pen down these final words, I want you to know that this journey, these words, haven't come easily. It has taken me over five years of battles, victories, and setbacks to muster the courage to share this story with you. The weight of my experiences, the depth of my pain, and the complexity of my struggles have been painstakingly etched onto these pages.

In the midst of this immense challenge, I discovered something profound: the power of resilience. It's not just my story but a testament to the human spirit's ability to endure, to persist, and to emerge stronger from the depths of despair. Every word you read is a triumph over the silence that once stifled me, a victory over the darkness that threatened to consume me.

The very act of putting pen to paper, of expressing what I have experienced, is a testament to the strength we can find within ourselves. It's a reminder that healing is not linear; it's a journey marked by twists and turns, ups and downs. And in sharing my story, I hope you find solace in your own journey, knowing that it's okay to take your time, to stumble, and to rise again.

As you close this book, carrying the weight of my words and the echoes of my experiences, remember that your path to healing is uniquely yours. It might take time – perhaps more time than you anticipated – but that doesn't diminish your strength or the validity of your struggles. You are not defined by your challenges; you are defined by your resilience, your ability to confront the darkness, and your determination to seek the light.

So, let these pages be a source of inspiration, a reminder that even in the face of seemingly insurmountable obstacles, you can find the strength to persevere. Your story, like mine, is a testament to your endurance, your bravery, and your unwavering spirit.

With profound gratitude for your journey and mine,

Brent Baldwin

Resources

National Suicide Prevention Lifeline Available 24/7, this helpline provides free and confidential support for people in distress, as well as prevention and crisis resources. Phone: **1-800-273-TALK** (1-800-273-8255)

Crisis Text Line Text **"HELLO" to 741741** to connect with a trained crisis counselor. This service is available 24/7 and provides free crisis intervention via SMS message.

Veterans Crisis Line Support for veterans and their loved ones, offering free, confidential support through phone, text, or chat. Phone: **1-800-273-8255** (Press 1) Text: 838255

NAMI Helpline (National Alliance on Mental Illness)NAMI offers information, referrals, and support to people living with mental health conditions and their families. Phone: **1-800-950-NAMI** (1-800-950-6264)

Substance Abuse and Mental Health Services Administration (SAMHSA)SAMHSA provides confidential and anonymous support for individuals and families facing substance abuse and mental health issues. Phone: **1-800-662-HELP** (1-800-662-4357)

Explore online therapy platforms like Better Help, Talkspace, or 7 Cups, where you can connect with licensed therapists through text, voice, or video calls.

Reach out to local mental health organizations in your

area. They often offer support groups, counseling services, and resources tailored to specific communities.

Books and Reading Materials Consider exploring literature related to mental health, anxiety, and depression. Books can provide valuable insights and coping strategies. Some recommended titles include "**The Noonday Demon**" by Andrew Solomon and "**Reasons to Stay Alive**" by Matt Haig.

Valor Bound Vets Support the cause by
visiting www.valorboundvets.com. Proceeds from
merchandise sold online contribute to funding
therapeutic trips for veterans suffering from mental
illnesses. Additionally, a portion of the proceeds from
every copy of this book sold will go towards the Valor
Bound Special Forces Team. This initiative enables
struggling veterans to embark on therapeutic journeys,
fostering healing and camaraderie.

Your support makes these programs possible, offering
a lifeline to those who have served and sacrificed.
Together, we can make a difference in the lives of our
veterans, providing them with the support and
resources they deserve.

Made in the USA
Middletown, DE
05 November 2023

41879835R00080